W9-CNR-924

by Victor Gentle and Janet Perry

Gareth Stevens Publishing
A WORLD ALMANAC EDUCATION GROUP COMPANY

Please visit our web site at: www.garethstevens.com
For a free color catalog describing Gareth Stevens Publishing's
list of high-quality books and multimedia programs,
call 1-800-542-2595 or fax your request to (414) 332-3567.

Library of Congress Cataloging-in-Publication Data

Gentle, Victor.
    Red foxes / by Victor Gentle and Janet Perry.
        p. cm. — (Wild dogs: an imagination library series)
    Includes bibliographical references and index.
    Summary: An introduction to the physical characteristics, behavior, and life cycle of red foxes,
small animals that are related to dogs.
    ISBN 0-8368-3098-9 (lib. bdg.)
    1. Red fox—Juvenile literature. [1. Red fox. 2. Foxes.] I. Perry, Janet. II. Title.
QL737.C22G447   2002
599.775—dc21   2001054993

First published in 2002 by
Gareth Stevens Publishing
A World Almanac Education Group Company
330 West Olive Street, Suite 100
Milwaukee, WI 53212 USA

Text: Victor Gentle and Janet Perry
Page layout: Victor Gentle, Janet Perry, and Tammy Gruenewald
Cover design: Tammy Gruenewald
Series editor: Catherine Gardner
Picture Researcher: Diane Laska-Swanke

Photo credits: Cover (main), pp. 5, 11, 13, 15, 19 © Alan & Sandy Carey; cover (background)
Diane Laska-Swanke; pp. 7, 17, 21 © Tom & Pat Leeson; p. 9 © Mark Hamblin/RSPCA Photolibrary

Printed in the United States of America

1 2 3 4 5 6 7 8 9 06 05 04 03 02

Front cover: Its fur is thick for winter, but this red fox is still light enough to stand on top of the snow for a good look around.

TABLE OF CONTENTS

Words that appear in the glossary are printed in **boldface**
type the first time they occur in the text.

FOX FABLES

Make-believe stories about red foxes might make you think that they are sneaky. In one story, Crow catches dinner and flies to a treetop to eat. Fox spots the chance for an easy meal and says to Crow, "People say you have a beautiful voice, but I've never heard it. Will you sing for me?" When Crow opens his mouth to sing, his dinner drops into Fox's hungry jaws.

True stories about real foxes show how clever they are. Real foxes are just smart enough to survive in a dangerous world.

This fox checks on a farmer's chickens. Foxes don't usually mess with humans, so this fox must be very hungry to risk hunting chickens in a farmer's pen.

REAL RED FOXES

Real red foxes use lots of tricks to help them get food. Some of their tricks sound like they came from a storybook.

For example, a red fox may trick a crow into becoming its supper! The fox plays dead and waits for a crow to land on it. When a crow lands, thinking it will make a meal out of the fox, the fox snatches the crow and eats it. That is a clever way to catch a meal!

This Alaskan fox carries a fancy meal, an arctic ground squirrel and a **ptarmigan**. Red foxes will carry food to a safe place or store it for later.

FOXY RED FOXES

Red foxes are not very big. They weigh as much as a large pet cat, and they are about as long and tall as a beagle. That is much smaller than the many **predators** that live alongside red foxes all over the world.

How do little red foxes survive when they must compete with much bigger predators, such as bears, coyotes, cougars, wolves, dingoes, vultures — or even humans?

To get enough food, foxes need to be clever about how they hunt and smart about what they eat.

This city fox digs in trash for tasty tidbits. Like rats and roaches, foxes have **adapted** to a world with less wilderness and more humans.

FOX FOOD

Foxes may choose foods other than small **prey**. They are willing to eat fruit, insects, dead animals, broken eggs, and human garbage. These foods are easy for red foxes to get and to **cache**. Red fox adults need about 2 pounds (1 kilogram) of food every day.

If red foxes find more food than they can eat at one time, they bury the rest for later. Dirt does not bother red foxes. After all, most of their favorite foods — **voles**, moles, ground squirrels, mice, and earthworms — live underground!

Gotcha! This fox grabs a very surprised pheasant for dinner. Fox legs are built like springs — the better to pounce with!

A FOX IS NOT A CAT

Red foxes have extra-strong senses of smell, sight, and hearing. They can smell old paw prints of a dog, see a rabbit's eye blinking in darkness, and hear earthworms crawling underground.

Foxes have whiskers, long **pupils** instead of round ones, **semi-retractable** claws, and fur padding on their feet. Cats also have these features, and they use them to hunt the same small prey as foxes.

But foxes are in the dog family, not the cat family.

Foxes and cats hunt the same prey in similar ways, so foxes seem "catlike" to us. This young fox plays with a dead ground squirrel, just as a cat might.

WHY IS A FOX A DOG?

Red foxes have certain features that most dogs have. Their leg bones are built to run long distances — way longer than any cat can. They have 42 teeth, while most cats have 30. Like other dogs, foxes have smooth tongues. Cats' tongues are rough. Like other dogs, red foxes can live alone or in groups.

Some groups have as many as eight red foxes. Most of them are sisters and daughters. One male and one female in the group, called the **mating pair**, have **cubs**. The rest hunt and babysit.

Forming groups can be hard for red foxes that live close to humans. This playful pair is lucky to have a home in the Montana wilderness.

PUFFS OF GRAY FOX FUR

The fox mating season begins in winter. A **vixen** (female) and a **dog fox** (male) meet, hunt, play, and sleep together every day. Then, for a few days in late winter, the vixen and dog fox mate.

The vixen finds a **den**, where she gives birth and hides her cubs. New red fox cubs are tiny, blind, and helpless gray puffs. They are about as heavy as three cookies. The father fox hunts food for the mother, so she can stay in the den, **nurse** the cubs, and keep them warm.

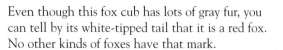

Even though this fox cub has lots of gray fur, you can tell by its white-tipped tail that it is a red fox. No other kinds of foxes have that mark.

CATCH AS CUBS CAN

Hunting lessons begin when cubs are a week old. The mother and father foxes drop mice in the den for the cubs to chew. Two-week-old cubs will wander into the wide world and play with anything they see.

The cubs stop nursing when they are five weeks old. Their parents leave prey outside the den to make the cubs search for it. Soon, the cubs go along on hunts, where they must catch their own food before they can eat.

For a year, young foxes learn survival skills alongside their parents. In the fall, they leave to find their own homes. Dog foxes go first, and vixens go later.

Red foxes' fur is not always red. It may be many colors, like red and gray, yellow, or even black. This black-coated red fox is called a silver fox.

LIVING DANGEROUSLY

The world is a dangerous place for young foxes. If they cross the **territory** of another fox, the other fox will attack them. Some predators think foxes make a good meal. Hunters trap and kill them. Farmers think foxes are pests and try to shoot them and poison them. But foxes eat crows, insects, and **rodents** that damage **crops**.

Many people think red foxes are too clever. But most foxes die before they are a year old because people kill them. Only the craftiest foxes are *clever enough* to survive. Are *we* smart enough to see a place for foxes in the wild?

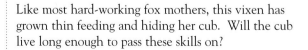

Like most hard-working fox mothers, this vixen has grown thin feeding and hiding her cub. Will the cub live long enough to pass these skills on?

MORE TO READ, VIEW, AND LISTEN TO

Books (Nonfiction) *City Foxes.* Susan J. Tweit (Alaska Northwest Books)
The Desert Fox Family Book. Animal Families (series).
   Hans Gerold Laukel (North-South)
Fox Magic for Kids. Animal Magic (series).
   Judy Schuler (Gareth Stevens)
Red Fox in Winter. First Start Science (series).
   Janet Craig (Troll Associates)
Wild Dogs (series). Victor Gentle and Janet Perry (Gareth Stevens)
Wild Fox. Cherie Mason (Down East Books)

Books (Fiction) *Aesop's Fox.* Aki Sogabe (Browndeer)
Fang: the Story of a Fox in Winter.
   Tessa Potter (Raintree Steck-Vaughn)

Books (Audio) *Wild Fox.* Cherie Mason (Audio Bookshelf)

PLACES TO VISIT, WRITE, OR CALL

Red foxes live at the following zoos. Call or write to the zoos to find out about their red foxes and their plans to preserve red foxes in the wild. Better yet, go see a red fox, person to dog!

Los Angeles Zoo
5333 Zoo Drive
Los Angeles, CA 90027-1498
(323) 644-6400

Papanack Zoo
150 Nine Mile Road
Wendover, Ontario, Canada KOA 3KO
(613) 673-PARK

Topeka Zoo
635 SW Gage Boulevard
Topeka, KS 66606
(785) 272-5821

WEB SITES

If you have your own computer and Internet access, great! If not, most libraries have Internet access. The Internet changes every day, and web sites come and go. We believe the following sites are likely to last and give the best, most appropriate links for readers to find out more about red foxes and other wild dogs around the world.

To get started finding web sites about red foxes, choose a general search engine. You can plug words into the search engine and see what it finds for you. Some words related to red foxes are: *foxes, red foxes, Vulpes vulpes, Australia, wild dogs, fox folk tales, den,* and *Britain wild life*.

www.google.com

Google is a huge search engine and a great research tool. Type in words such as *foxes, red foxes, canids, wild dogs,* and *fox folk tales* to find all kinds of information about red foxes and everywhere they live in the world.

www.animalpicturesarchive.com/animal/ SOUND

At the *Animal Pictures Archive*, you can listen to all kinds of animals sounding off! Compare a fox to a leopard, or a whale to a wolf. There are also tons of great pictures of foxes.

www.enchantedlearning.com/subjects/ mammals/fox

At *Enchanted Learning*, you will find virtual coloring pages, games, puzzles, and more about red foxes, where they live, and the animals

they compete with, such as coyotes, wolves, dingoes, lynxes, and arctic foxes.

www.foxbox.org/

When you get to *Adam's Fox Box*, click on Gallery, then on Fox Vox (audio/video), and you will get to a page with lots of videos and fox sounds — in a few formats, too, so you will probably be in luck and find one that works with the computer you use.

www.nationalgeographic.com/features/ 97/cats/

National Geographic has the plans for a perfect predator. They say it is the cat, but foxes have some of the same features as cats! Click on skeleton and then on claw to see the retractable claw in action. Also, click on senses and then on eye, pupil, and whiskers!

www.ozfoxes.com/aafoxes.htm

The *OzFoxes FoxWeb* has all kinds of interesting facts about foxes, including how to say "fox" in 35 languages, from Choctaw to Spanish.

GLOSSARY

You can find these words on the pages listed. Reading a word in a sentence helps you understand it even better.

adapted (uh-DAPT-ed) — changed ways of doing things to fit in better in a place 8

cache (KASH) — hide or store food 10

crops (KRAHPS) — plants grown on farms 20

cubs (KUHBS) — baby foxes 14, 16, 18, 20

den (DEN) — place where some animals give birth, hide their young, and sleep 16, 18

dog fox (DAWG FAHKS) — adult male fox 16, 18

mating pair (MAYT-ing PAIR) — the only male and female animals in a pack that come together to have young 14

nurse (NURS) — to feed milk to cubs 16, 18

predators (PRED-uh-turs) — animals that hunt other animals for food 8, 20

prey (PRAY) — animals that are hunted by other animals for food 10, 12, 18

ptarmigan (TAR-mi-guhn) — an arctic bird that looks like a grouse with feathered feet 6

pupils (PYOU-puhlz) — black parts of the eyes that allow light in for vision 12

rodents (ROHD-uhnts) — small animals like beavers, mice, squirrels, moles, and voles 20

semi-retractable (SEM-ee re-TRAK-tuh-buhl) — able to draw back halfway into a paw 12

territory (TER-uh-tor-ee) — area of land that an animal (or a group of animals) marks out as its hunting ground 20

vixen (VIK-suhn) — female fox 16, 18, 20

voles (VOHLZ) — small mouse-like animals that have dark fur and live underground 10

INDEX

24